THE GPS GUIDE TO SUCCESS:

How to Navigate Life to Reach Your
Personal and Career Goals

REVIEWS

"This handbook is clear and easy to read. Alex does an excellent job of explaining a new type of GPS without bombarding the reader with industry-filled jargon. In less than a day, you can read this handbook, reexamine your goals, and develop new strategies to meet your goals. Anyone who is goal oriented and aspiring to become a successful leader in any industry should read this handbook."

—*Priscilla Kucer*, *Ph.D., School Psychologist*

"A simple but meaningful tool to assist anyone in the pursuit of their life goals. The metaphor of a GPS system, along with roadblocks, pit stops, and detours, is an excellent way for individuals to follow and follow through. Enjoyable reading with pertinent examples. A good read for literally anyone—whether you are just deciding where you want to be or are a seasoned professional who needs a 'jump start' to get you motivated again."

—*Marci Ronik*, *M.S., Principal Partner, The Ronik-Radlauer Group*

"This handbook emphasizes to the readers that asking 'why,' not just 'what,' is very important when they develop their career goals. It also encourages the readers to recognize that there might be detours and traffic even when they build concrete plans and strategies, and that is okay.

Alex provides not only a practical tool, but also insightful advice to those who like to start thinking about their ultimate career goals and wonder how to get there."

—Jung Ran Lim, M.A., Senior Director, Academic Internship
Programs and International Development

"I appreciate the work of the author in this useful handbook. Everyone could talk about the content discussed in this handbook, but I think few people could explain it as simply and as clear as the author of *The GPS Guide to Success.*"

—S. Hossein Jalali, Ph.D., Strategy and Management
Consultant

"This is a MUST read for anyone who wants to succeed. *The GPS Guide to Success* gives directions about how one can reach one's goals. It teaches the reader the importance of asking the right questions: What is the objective and why is this the objective and how to map the way there, given that nothing is a straight line."

—Regis Cabral, Ph.D., Director, FEPRO—*Funding for
European Projects*

"In *The GPS Guide to Success*, Alex Tremble provides a process that acts as a guidance system for determining where you want to go, how you will get there, and how to stay on course. This easily digestible handbook reassures readers that they can indeed reach their goals and motivates them to take the first step."

—Elizabeth Stincelli, D.M., Founder, Stincelli Advisors

"This is a handbook for young professionals who are starting their career and are serious about reaching their goals and dreams. It outlines a practical, straightforward methodology which can apply in virtually any situation. The author has written this manual as a means of sharing with other young professionals his own experience in achieving success early in his career. What struck me was how the principles outlined—defining a goal, setting a timeline, asking 'why,' and so forth—are not unique. Certainly this is not the first book to be written on how to achieve personal success. What it does is pull out the most fundamental concepts in a clear, easy-to-understand manner. In fact, I found it to be a useful reminder for how to address a personal dream I have had for a long time but have not made satisfactory progress. Even if I am a little older than the intended audience, I also found this handbook to be valuable."

—*Steffen Eckart*, M.A., *Human Resources Professional*

"Never has so much been said so comprehensively. I loved how he has taken only 36 pages to compile enough energy in a person to start off any goal, be it big or small."

—*Benish Chaudhry*, Ph.D., *University Instructor*

ACKNOWLEDGMENTS

————◆————◆————◆————

I would like to begin by thanking God. Without God and the challenges he has allowed me to overcome, I would not be the person I am today. Without God I would not have come in contact with the many family members, friends, and mentors who pushed me to always do better. I would also like to acknowledge my wonderful girlfriend, Su Hlaing Win Nu, for serving as my first reviewer and being patient with me as I dedicated most of my free time to undertaking this writing project.

I am blessed to have an army of extremely experienced, knowledgeable, and accomplished mentors who truly care about me and my success. Their invaluable feedback on earlier versions of this handbook led to the successful completion of this book project. Thank you Eric Barger, Sherketta Carter, Dutch Driver, Ann Fields, Jerry Gidner, Tony Johnson, Kriste Jordan, Mary Ma, Steve Noah, Rene Redwood, Rich Rischling, Slagjana Stojanovska, and Kitty Wooley. I would also like to thank Douglas Garland Jr., Kirin Kennedy, Andrew Lee, Janice Mompoint, and many other friends who continue to stay by my side in motivating and encouraging me to strive for the best.

I would like to thank my wonderful family for supporting me in all of my endeavors. My awesome siblings (Angela, Jasper, Monique, Unique, and Z'nara), my beautiful parents (Johnny and Robin), my phenomenal grandparents (Alexander, Darleen, and Martha), and my brilliant cousin (Aja Trotter) have always encouraged me to be a better person and to put others before me. Finally, I would like to thank you, the reader, for making the decision to use your valuable time to read this handbook. I am certain that you will take away something positive and useful from this guide, and I look forward to receiving your feedback.

I'd also like to thank the individuals listed below for their essential role in completing this handbook. They volunteered their time and efforts to review this book because of their passion for helping others achieve their goals. I look forward to future collaboration with them.

Adriana Schiopoiu Burlea	Allen Onu-Njoku
Romania	*Indonesia*
Benish Chaudhry	Ciaran Moore
United Arab Emirates	*Ireland*
Dr. Brent Stephens	Dr. Elizabeth Stincelli
United States	*United States*
Elizabeth Jayanti	Mary Hormozzadeh
United States	*Iran*
Mustafa Topcu	Regis Cabral
Turkey	*Sweden*
Robert Haughton	Rula Al-Abdulrazak
United States	*United Kingdom*
S. Jalali Hossein	Shakil Khan
Iran	*United States*
Steffen Eckart	Stephen G. Ruby
Japan	*United States*
Susan E. Murray	Vladimir Damnjanovic
Canada	*Serbia*
Priscilla Kucer	Ross Nichols
United States	*United Kingdom*
Ahmad Duranai	Reginald Hubbard
Canada	*United States*
Marci Ronik	Rebecca Riffle
United States	*United States*
Jung Ran Lim	Xuefang Liu
United States	*China*
Sharre A. Brooks	Michael J. D. Sutton
United States	*United States*
Mustafa Kemal	S. Hossein Jalali
Turkey	*Iran*

Table of Contents

INTRODUCTION

W ith over 50% of the U.S. workforce eligible for retirement within the next few years (and similar numbers around the world) and a projected worldwide shortage of qualified workers, young professionals are presented with a rare opportunity to assume leadership roles earlier in their careers than their predecessors. However, in order to take advantage of this opportunity, they must begin to develop their leadership skills *today*.

For the last 3 years, I served as one of the youngest federal government employees to manage an agency-wide executive leadership development program. During my time in that role, I had the great honor of meeting and learning from some of the world's renowned thought leaders (e.g., Marshall Goldsmith, executive coach and author of *What Got You Here Won't Get You There*, and Admiral Thad Allen, who oversaw the rescue and clean-up efforts for Hurricane Katrina), speaking at multiple conferences, serving as an international liaison, and shaking the hand of the U.S. President Barack Obama. Though some have labeled me as "lucky," I believe that we can all achieve our goals as long as we have the right tools. My Goals, Plans, and Strategies (GPS) were the tools I used to make my own luck a reality.

After facilitating a workshop at the Future Business Leaders of America Conference in 2012, I was asked to write a briefing paper on the GPS Success Model so that it could be shared with others who were unable to attend. What started as a short article eventually grew into a comprehensive guide highlighting the importance of defining goals, creating specific plans, and using creative strategies to ensure the success of our plans. This practical handbook will provide you with concepts and strategies that can be easily implemented in your day-to-day life.

This handbook offers a number of very effective tools for identifying and attaining career and life success. I intentionally made this handbook short and to the point. It is my goal to have you spend your time implementing the strategies. As this is not an exhaustive list of strategies, once you finish reading, please feel free to share with me any additional strategies that you believe will help others. No one knows everything, so it is up to us to teach and share what we know with our friends, family members, and colleagues, wherever they may be. I hope you enjoy your read and share your strategies as well.

HOW GPS WAS CREATED

hroughout my life, I have been afforded many wonderful opportunities to be mentored by various caring, intelligent, and respected professionals. These mentors came from extremely diverse industries, such as international business and chief learning officers in the federal government, to political pollsters and high school counselors. Of the many lessons they taught me, one of the most important has been the need to clearly establish, define, and pursue goals—particularly, my academic and professional goals. Over time, I realized that not only did my goals evolve as I grew, but my idea of what a goal meant changed as well. In high school, my first goals were playing college football and becoming a lawyer. Next, I dreamed of becoming a military pilot. By high school graduation, I had decided that I wanted to become a high school counselor, so that I could help other youth as my mentors had helped me.

During college and graduate school, my goals changed drastically. Accompanying these changes were feelings of anxiety and uncertainty. I still remember the last semester of my junior year at William Penn University. Like most colleges, Penn required all students to take a list of particular courses before they could graduate. Knowing that I wanted to become a high school counselor, I had proactively taken almost every psychology and sociology course the school had to offer and now was registered in what was called "Contemporary Leadership." This course was my first introduction to business operations and the concept of leadership and its effects on employees. Not 3 weeks into the class, I fell in love with this topic. I struggled with this because I knew that I wanted to be a counselor so that I could help children. What I once thought I knew was no longer a certainty. My future suddenly felt unknown and out of reach.

For the entire semester, I was locked in an internal struggle over whether I should still become a counselor or shift my sights to the business world. Fortunately, **this tension was eased once I realized that goals are fluid,** changing with one's personal development and experiences. I also realized that by finding a position in a company that would allow me to be a mentor, I could still help youth succeed in life. However, each time I created a plan to achieve my goals, **it became fairly easy to see how stress of the unknown** (i.e., not knowing what I wanted in life) **could cause so much anxiety**. Each time I thought I knew what my goal was and created a plan to attain it, I would have a new experience causing me to change my goal and have to start over. This pattern continued **until I reconceptualized my idea of a "goal," which allowed me to finally program my GPS.**

WHAT IS THE GPS SUCCESS MODEL?

Have you wondered why others get ahead and you don't? Are you struggling with your career and still don't know where you want to be? What steps will you need to take to get there? What does "there" even look like? If you find you're asking yourself questions such as these, this is the handbook for you!

When most people refer to the acronym "GPS," they are typically referring to the widely used global positioning system, famous for strategically navigating its user through the many streets and highways we travel on a daily basis. However, I have found the acronym to be much more useful when strategically navigating through the challenges, split decisions, and uncertainty I encounter in life. This handbook will provide you with your own personal and professional GPS, with easy directions to guide you to the success you want to achieve.

Just like driving through the open roads or the densely populated cities we live in today, it is easy to feel lost in life. The many one-way streets, roundabouts, freeways, and back roads can confuse and disorientate even the most focused individuals. But, like these roads, life can be easily navigated with the right tools. The **Goals, Plans, and Strategies (GPS) success model provides the tools to map a credible route to achieve goals (i.e., end destination) and "recalculate" when we have reached an unexpected detour.** Like a GPS, when we find ourselves at a closed road, we must be able to reroute so that we can continue in the direction of our end destination.

Life Is Not a Highway

Life is not a two-lane highway; it more closely resembles a densely populated city. When traveling through a city, very seldom can a destination be reached without making at least one turn. Even if there were no detours or road blocks on our trip, we would still have to make a "left turn here" or a "right turn there" to reach our destination. This is because not only is it in our best interest to move forward, to the right, to the left, and, yes, at times a few steps back, but sometimes it is necessary to move up a level (increase our resources) or strategically move down a level (use a lower technical ability). To move up a level is to increase strategic complexity, effort, and resources, whereas to move down a level is to decrease the amount of strategic complexity, effort, and resources.

For example, my office building has 10 levels, and my office is on the fourth floor. To get to the cafeteria, I have to go down four levels, make two left turns, and make one right turn to reach my destination. To relate this to life, sometimes we may feel that we have arrived at a certain level in life or our job. Because of this, we feel that all of our strategies should be consistent with that level as well. The level we believe we are on (e.g., college student, entry level, mid level, or executive) directly influences whom we identify with and collaborate with. However, just as there are times when we work at a higher level than where we presently believe we are (e.g., trying to stand out for a promotion or impress the new boss, showing true passion about a particular project and its outcome), there are times when less effort is appropriate (i.e., costs outweigh the possible benefits). Finally, we should remember that though getting to the cafeteria requires us to follow a specific set of directions, the path to reaching the cafeteria is totally different for someone in a different building, on a different floor, in a different office, or requiring special accommodations.

It is also beneficial to maintain the networks and relationships built at each level. Most people would agree that cultivating relationships at the senior levels is a must to achieve career success. However, just as the individuals at senior levels have a certain amount of influence, so do the individuals at the lower levels. In fact, these people tend to have much more influence than most people think. Take an administrative assistant, for example. This job may be seen as low level, but administrative assistants control the executive's schedule, who is able to contact the executive, and what tasks are prioritized. The same holds true for many positions such as the budget officer, IT worker, janitor, and countless others.

Traffic

Like driving a car in heavy traffic, there are times when we are simply stuck. We may have chosen the right road to reach our destination, but we are being slowed down by any number of reasons (e.g., the boss will not support career growth, a bad economy, or too many people fighting for the same resources). At this point it becomes important to ask ourselves, "Is timing important?" If not, we may choose to wait patiently. However, if timing is important, it may be in our best interest to reassess our situation and find an alternate route.

Finding Short Cuts

All too often, people look for short cuts to get where they want to be, but it is important to realize that the best route is not always the shortest. This is not to say that all short cuts are bad, but that there are good reasons for taking the longer route sometimes. It is critical to assess both the risks and benefits of each possible route.

For example, you need to arrive at destination B within 4 hours to meet with some old friends. The first route will get you there in 4 hours, while the second route will get you there in 2 hours. Which route will you take? You then find out that the second route is much shorter because it is a back road, with no gas stations, and is said to be unsafe. Are there benefits to arriving on time versus 2 hours early? Is the risk worth taking? The point is that it is always in the best interest of the driver to assess the risks and benefits of each possible route. Just because one road to your goal may take longer does not mean that that road is not the best one for you to take.

Withholding Judgment

Because we are all going different places using different modes of transportation, it does not make sense to compare ourselves to, or make judgments, of other people. Think about it. Is a sports car better than a Jeep because it can beat the Jeep in a street race? Would the results be the same if the race took place in a sand dune? Furthermore, to judge another vehicle on the road by its exterior is not helpful either. To think that we are closer to reaching our destination than another driver because our car is cleaner, more expensive, or is moving faster at that particular time is naive and ignorant. We do not know if that car is moving at full speed or not, how long that car has been traveling, if that person is just learning how to drive, or if it was recently vandalized for no reason. Because we do not know this information, it is safer and smarter to not judge at all.

Special Features

Finally, as we drive down life's roads, it is important to recognize that we are all driving different vehicles (e.g., Jeeps, sports vehicles, muscle cars, motorcycles, etc.) with unique and special features. Even if we see a vehicle that looks similar to ours, there is no way to know what features that vehicle may have. We must remember that though we are traveling on the same roads, we are all driving to different destinations with different modes of transportation and different starting points. Like our vehicles, we are unique and come with our own special features. The trick is, instead of focusing on the features we *think* the vehicle next to us has, we should focus on identifying our own strengths and using them to our advantage. If we have great interpersonal skills, we should find ways to leverage those skills to help us succeed. The same thing goes for people who are detail-oriented, are social media geniuses, or are natural problem solvers. **If you have a Jeep that came with mud tires, don't limit yourself to driving on the freeway because you see others doing it.** *Go off road!*

IDENTIFYING STRATEGIC GOALS

Understanding *why* we want something is the first step to achieving success.

The Importance of Why

Why is one of the most powerful questions in the universe and is the foundation of goal creation. To show just how important *why* is, the section below briefly presents an argument made by Simon Sinek (2009) on <u>TED Talks</u>.

<u>Sinek</u> (2009) began his talk by asking a number of questions: Why was Martin Luther King Jr. such an inspirational leader? Why is Apple Inc. so much more innovative than its competitors? Why were the Wright Brothers able to figure out controlled power-manned flight when others who were better financed were unable to do so? In each of these examples, there were others who could have been just as successful at that time, but did not succeed. Simon then explained that these successful individuals had the ability to think the exact opposite of how most people think. These individuals all had a compelling *why* behind their desire to succeed.

Sinek (2009) explained that most people begin a task by first deciding *what* they want to accomplish. This is then followed by *how* they will accomplish the *what* (Figure 1). Very few individuals take the time to decide *why* they want something. For example, Ford makes trucks (what) and builds them with material strong enough to haul very heavy loads (how); therefore, people should buy Ford trucks (why). Apple, on the other hand, starts by defining *why* it exists (e.g., to create products of the utmost quality that are user friendly), then explains the *how* (by focusing a substantial amount of resources in R&D and strongly promoting innovation). The *what* then becomes a byproduct of the *why* and *how*. Apple and others have found that beginning the thought process by asking *what* can limit creativity by making the mind focus on a specific result. In Ford's case, because it focused only on how to build vehicles, all of its ideas would be limited to how to improve vehicles (specifically, vehicles with four wheels and the normal framework). In contrast, because Apple's focus is much broader (i.e., creating aesthetically pleasing user-friendly technology), its innovation has led it to create computers, phones, radios, applications, and much more. Can you see the power of a contemplating *why* before you get to *how* or *what*?

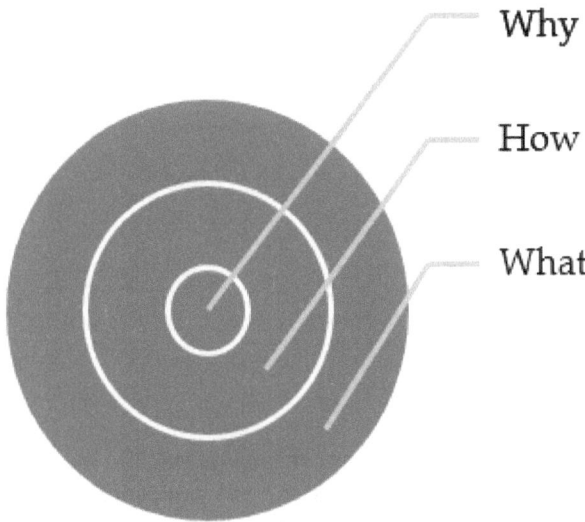

Figure 1. The golden circle. Adapted from Sinek, September 2009.

Appling Why to Your Goals

Have you ever gone on a road trip or driven a long distance to reach a destination? When you were planning the trip, you most likely knew your starting point (Point A) and where you would end up (Point B). While on the road to your destination, you might have stopped at a restaurant, a gas station, a rest stop, or a tourist stop (i.e., pit stops), but the likelihood of you planning to stop at that specific restaurant, gas station, or rest stop was pretty slim. In fact, most people choose which pit stops to rest at by what is around them when they need to stop. Even if you had planned on making those pit stops, you did so knowing you would only be there for a short amount of time because your ultimate goal was to reach Point B. This is not to say those places were not important (we all know how important fuel is), but your main focus was, and should have been, your end destination. Pit stops are not necessarily "bad." In fact, they can help us stay focused and energized while on our trip. However, we must always make sure our pit stops serve a purpose and are of value to us.

> *Asking yourself "why" you want to create something rather than "what" you want to create allows the mind to be much more creative when exploring options.*

Now, let's apply this same thinking to real life. We may know where we are now, but what is our end destination? How do we differentiate the end destination from the pit stops? How can we stay on course of reaching our end destination with all of life's challenges that may detour or obstruct us? This is where asking *why* becomes so important.

Begin by asking yourself what your goal is. You may initially answer this question by focusing on the *what*—identifying things such as getting a degree, receiving a promotion, becoming a partner at a firm, or making a certain salary. This is normal because society encourages us to focus on the *what*. Once you have decided on a goal, ask yourself: "**Why is that my goal?**" or "**Why is that important?**" (Figure 2). Once you have answered these questions, ask yourself the same two questions regarding your answer. Continue to ask yourself those two questions until you cannot ask why anymore. This process can sometimes be difficult to perform yourself, so it may help to ask a friend or mentor to walk you through the process.

For example, the average college student might identify his or her goal as graduating from college. If asked why that is important, he or she may reply "to get a good job." When further questioned, he or she may reply "to receive a higher salary." When asked why a high salary is important, he or she may reply "to purchase a nice house." When asked why a nice house is important, the individual may respond, "Because my family needs a safe, comfortable place to live." This example elucidates the student's end destination: to provide a safe and comfortable place for the family to live. This could be taken further and the student may respond "Because I am family oriented."

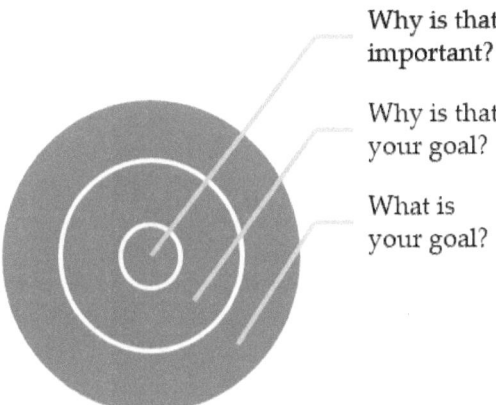

Why is that important?

Why is that your goal?

What is your goal?

Figure 2. Identifying your end destination.

At this point, you have most likely identified your end destination. This can be anything, but in my experience working with individuals using this model, you have probably identified something outcome oriented, such as being able to take care of your family, being able to travel the world, living "comfortably," being able to give back to the community, or being able to provide an avenue for children to escape poverty.

There are many benefits to identifying an end destination (or ultimate goal) that is outcome oriented. First and foremost, once you distinguish an outcome, goals tend to be more stable and can be achieved in many ways. For instance, the probability of an individual wanting to become a partner at a specific firm and then 2 years later moving to another company and wanting something completely different is much higher than an individual wanting to take care of his or her family and then 2 years later deciding that his or her family is no longer important. By thinking through the *why* of a goal, the stability of the end destination is increased. Secondly, these types of goals are achieved over a lifetime, which allows the individual to always have something to strive for. An example of a short-term goal versus an end destination is graduating from college versus helping to ensure children are not living in poverty. In addition, outcome-oriented goals help successful people see new opportunities that they could otherwise miss if they only had a short-term goal in mind.

On the way to becoming a partner in a law firm, for instance, a person is presented with two possible career paths. If the end destination is clear, the individual will have the flexibility to seize opportunities and know which path will lead there sooner—but only if the GPS is initially set with that long-term goal in mind.

To reinforce the importance of goal stability, consider the fact that individuals change jobs an average of 11 times during life. [1] Now imagine this person going on a road trip and the GPS sending him to

---

[1] U.S. Bureau of Labor Statistics,
www.bls.gov/nls/nlsy79r23jobsbyedu.pdf.

11 different locations before he reaches his destination. This would most likely cause feelings of anxiety, frustration, and confusion, not to mention a loss of valuable time. But, if the individual realizes that those 11 stops were on a path of greater purpose, he or she may be more likely to see such changes as beneficial rather than disruptive.

> *Overspecifying a goal can unnecessarily restrict creativity and cause anxiety when the specific goal cannot be reached.*

The Benefits of Asking Why

The benefits of asking *why* are twofold:

1. We gain a new *awareness* of ourselves and our desires. We are now conscious of what we value the most in our lives. Having a clear understanding of the importance of a particular goal and what underlies the pursuit of this goal will likely increase our motivation and effort put forth in attaining benchmarks and reaching our goals (Figure 3).

2. Establishing a *stable goal* tied to a value should allow us to be more resilient and creative in instances of unforeseen challenges. This rationale stems from the notion that having a more outcome-oriented goal, which is not linked to a particular field of interest, will allow us to think outside of the box when faced with a challenge (Figure 3). For example, if Tom's goal is to become a partner at ABC law firm and he is fired, he is faced with limited options to meet this goal (i.e., get rehired at the same firm). If the goal becomes too difficult to attain, he may be forced to start over and identify a new goal.

However, if his end destination is to provide his family with a house in a safe neighborhood, he could quickly reassess his skills, network to arrive at an alternative method for attaining his ultimate goal, and therefore *reduce the anxiety* associated with limited options.

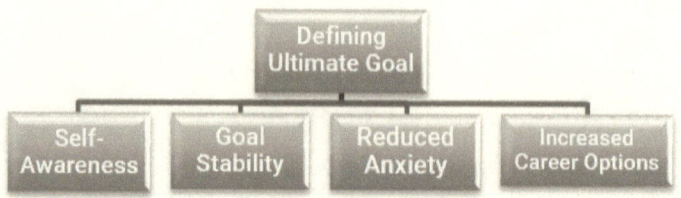

Figure 3. Defining your ultimate goal.

The difference in the two options is that Tom's first goal (partner at the ABC law firm) is highly specific and ultimately limits the number of possible options. Simply redefining the goal to "becoming a partner at a law firm" rather than at a specific law firm would have provided Tom more flexibility and *increased career options*. This is not to say that Tom would not have eventually come up with an alternative option, but because of the self-imposed constraints, he will most likely experience a greater amount of anxiety for a longer amount of time.

CREATING EFFECTIVE PLANS

Once successful people have used the *why* to figure out where they want to go (i.e., identified an end destination), the next step is to figure out *how* to get there.

Setting a Timeline

The first step in developing a plan is to employ the *"X to Y by when"* principle.[2] In this equation, "X" is where we are now, "Y" is where we want to be, and "when" sets the time restraints. A timeline is essential to any plan because it allows successful people to know if they are running late, on time, or early in nearing completion of their designated tasks.

"In preparing for battle I have always found that plans are useless, but planning is indispensable."
—Dwight D. Eisenhower, 34th President of the United States

---

[2] FranklinCovey.com/tc/public/images/books/tools/chapter1.pdf.

For example, imagine that your supervisor assigns you two tasks, each taking a week to complete. Task A is due in a week, but Task B is not given a due date. Which task will you complete first? A week passes and you have successfully completed Task A and are working on Task B. Now your supervisor assigns you an additional task (Task C) that is due in 1 week. What task will you complete first? What task will you complete last? If the trend of task assignments continues, there is a strong probability that Task B will never be completed. This is because people associate time restraints with importance. If we set a goal but do not establish time restraints, it becomes easy to push the goals to a later date in order to make time for tasks that are "more important." Having time restraints also provides us with additional motivation due to a greater sense of urgency.

Backwards Planning—Planning from the Future

Backwards planning is the process of beginning with an established goal that has specific time constraints, then identifying each action (i.e., milestone and pit stop) that must be completed in order to reach the goal by the specified date. Milestones are the initial tasks that need to be completed before reaching a pit stop, whereas pit stops are the specific accomplishments required (or believed to be required) to reach the end destination. This may sound difficult, but it is actually a simple and effective tool. Once the pit stops are identified, a list of milestones that will help us reach the pit stops must be created. Because most ultimate goals will require more than one action, an effective plan may have multiple layers of pit stops.

For example, if a successful person has identified her end destination and believes that owning one of the world's leading real estate companies is a pit stop she must reach before progressing to the end destination, she may identify the first pit stops as attaining a real estate license and getting a mentor (Figure 4). Some milestones may be researching possible real estate license courses and networking on Linkedin.com™. Once all possible milestones are identified, the individual should create a list of action steps that must be taken to attain the milestone. The additional benefit of setting a milestone schedule is that it helps successful people prioritize what comes first.

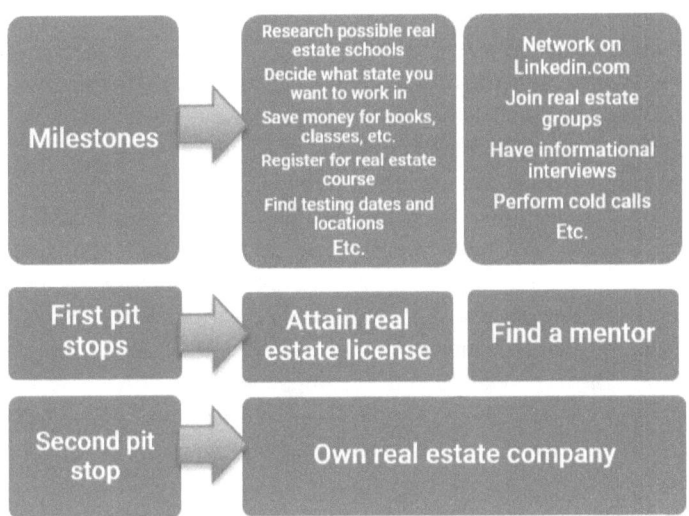

Figure 4. Milestone and pit stop example.

Now that we have identified our *why*, pit stops, milestones, and time constraints, we can begin the process of planning backwards. Using the example above, if the individual wants to achieve the second-level pit stop of owning a real estate company within 2 years, she would likely want to reach her milestones within 6 months and primary pit stops in a year. At this step it is important that your plan is simple, specific, realistic, and complete. All too often plans fail because they are needlessly complex, impractical, too general, or incomplete.

Be Simple, Specific, Realistic, and Complete

When a plan is overly complex, the probability of something going wrong increases dramatically. Consider, as an example, giving driving directions to friends who have never been to your house, or even your town. While providing them with detailed instructions through the many back roads of your town may save them a few minutes, they run the risk of getting lost. Keep it simple and give them the highway directions instead.

Though we should set challenging goals, it is important to also be realistic. A realistic plan is distinguished from an unrealistic plan by the probability and possibility of it succeeding (improbable vs. impossible). For example, a federal employee decided that his end destination was to attain a position where he could positively influence the lives of all Americans. To achieve this goal, he identified a number of pit stops, one being attaining public office. He then identified a few milestones that included volunteering for campaigns, becoming more active in his community, and getting a mentor. Aside from those milestones, he also included a milestone solely for the purpose of motivation. This employee wanted to meet the president of the United States of America. To accomplish this, the individual planned to volunteer at every event the president might attend. An alternate way of accomplishing the goal of meeting the president was to jump over the White House fence, run towards the front door, enter the building, and find the president. This may seem like an extreme method, but someone tried doing just that during the summer of 2012. Needless to say, that individual did not make it far.

This is where one learns the difference between impossible and improbable. Neither approach is impossible; that is, the individual could physically perform both options. However, the second approach is highly improbable. The probability of the individual making it over the fence, passing the Secret Service, getting into the house, and finding the president is slim to none. Though this may be an extreme example, the premise stands. When creating a plan, and assuming we have our *why* in order, we must be sure to take into consideration the probability of the plan actually working. Not sure if a plan is credible? Ask someone you trust (e.g., a mentor) to help you create a carefully thorough plan. The notion of being realistic also involves time constraints and is why planning backwards is important. If we decide that we want to reach a goal in 6 months, but each identified milestone takes a total of 8 months to complete, it may be necessary to reassess the goal or the estimated completion date.

Finally, a good plan is specific and complete. A plan that is general or incomplete allows room for error that can cause failure. Read the two set of directions below. Both sets of instructions are directions to my aunt's house.

A. You are going to drive a while until you pass a parking lot next to a big tree where you are going to turn. Head down the street until you see a house with a blue roof.

B. You need to drive down Broadway Street for about 6 miles where you will reach a toll road. The toll will cost you $3.00. One mile after you pass the toll, make a right on K Street and you will arrive at 1984 K Street on the left.

Which set of directions is easier to follow? Is there a chance that you may get lost, turned around, or at least delayed if you were to follow the first set of directions? Just like having specific and complete directions is beneficial when traveling, having a specific and complete plan for reaching your goal is crucial to success. Instead of going through life knowing that a turn needs to be made, but not knowing when or where, successful people can be confident that they have taken the right actions because they identified the most important aspects of their journey: distance, street names, and toll roads.

Knowing the Distance. Similar to planning backwards, distance refers to the time needed to reach the next turn or the destination. By knowing approximately how long it should take to reach any particular point, successful people can be confident that they are either on track for reaching their destination or conscious of a possible missed turn. Recognizing that they should have reached the next turn in 3 months but it has already been 6 months, they can reassess where they are and focus their energy on finding their next off ramp (i.e., next path to achieving the goal). For example, an individual wants to become a realtor. How often is the real estate license exam offered? If the exam is offered monthly, then there may be ample opportunities to take the exam. However, if the exam is offered only annually or semiannually, the individual needs to plan how close he or she is to the next offering and take into consideration the extra time needed if an exam date has just passed.

Knowing the Street Names. Knowing the distance to a particular location provides successful people with an estimation of how long it should take to reach their next turn, while knowing the street name assures that they turn at the correct place. A street name is a specific action or place where a resource is and allows successful people to be confident that they are making the right choice when the opportunity arises. Using the realtor example, the individual knows when the exams are offered and now must know where they are offered. Is there a location that is closer than others, has a higher pass rate, more prestige, etc.? These are all important questions to consider to make sure that the correct street is identified.

Knowing the Toll Roads. Successful people take the time to identify tolls roads before they are confronted with one. By taking the time to identify the potential cost associated with the potential paths to success, they are able to strategically decide which path to take by weighing the pros and cons. For example, is a particular path less expensive than another? What are the benefits of the more expensive path? Can they afford either path? If not, how long will it take to raise the money?

The most important benefit of having goals that are complete and specific is that individuals know if they are, at least, in the right vicinity of their goals. That is, if they do run into a road block or detour, they can easily reorient themselves to get back on the path to success.

IMPLEMENTING CREATIVE STRATEGIES

I n the strategy stage, successful people explore the bounds of their imagination and decide what techniques they will use to reach the destination. In this handbook, strategies refer to creating and broadening one's network of influence and finding creative ways to engage in self-development.

To those who want to be successful: Know where you are going and make a good plan to get there. To do this, follow the model in Figure 5 and focus on the four steps to achieve success. Once you have identified your goal(s) (i.e., end destination), you can put yourself in situations where you are around others who share your interests. This by no means suggests that it is not important to socialize with individuals who have different interests than you. Once you are in the company of those with shared interests, you will need to work hard to meet those who can help you succeed. Do your best, be kind, and take responsibility for your actions. If you can accomplish this and focus on your goal, you may ultimately reach career success.

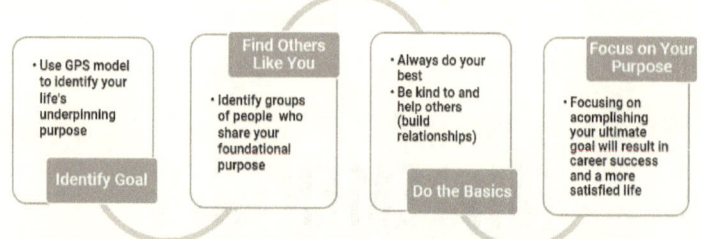

Figure 5. The golden path.

For example, take a look at the conversation that I had with a young lady named Julie:

Julie: Alex, how do I know what my ultimate goal is, and how do I know what career is for me?

Alex: What do you really want to do in your life?

Julie: Build a library in my native country.

Alex: Why do you want to do that?

Julie: Because I want to give children the opportunity to learn.

Alex: Why do you want them to have the opportunity to learn?

Julie: Because they should have the opportunity to dream and achieve those dreams.

Alex: So it seems that providing children with the opportunity to learn and achieve their dreams is what is really important to you.

At that point she had an epiphany:

Julie: So I don't have to just build a library! There are so many things I can do that will achieve that goal.

Next, Julie asked me, "Well, how do I know what career to start?" I responded:

Alex: Now that you know what you really want to do, you should find others who are passionate about helping children learn. This could be meet-up groups, social websites, or organizations. All that really matters is that you are around others doing work in the area you care about and that their *whys* are aligned with your *why*. Once you find those groups, start to volunteer and build relationships with the members of the group. This will show them the quality of your work, reaffirm your passion, and build relationships that can lead to future job offers. Finally, you will find that if you are working hard, presenting a good product, and are genuinely nice and helpful to others, you will work your way up the ladder. The great thing about building relationships with people in your area of interest is that they most likely know others in that area who you do not yet know. And as I have experienced in my life, your name will travel through the ranks quickly if you are doing good work.

Julie has since gone on to volunteer for many organizations and has been introduced to a number of senior leaders who actively mentor her and search for ways to help her reach her goals.

The concept of strategy also applies to the behaviors we engage in. For this reason, I have included three of the most important tips I have come across from my mentors, reading books, attending trainings, and my personal life experiences (Figure 6):

- o   Self-development
- o   Find a support network
- o   Take responsibility for decisions

Career Strategies		
Self-Development	**Find a Support Network**	**Take Responsibility for Decisions**
No one is more responsible for your career than you. Find ways to learn more about yourself and develop your leadership and technical skills regardless of your organization's willingness to invest in you.	Build relationships with individuals who want you to succeed and/or are interested in areas that are important for your success.	Always take responsibility for your actions. Doing this will build others' trust and respect for you.

Figure 6. Three easy career strategies.

Career Tip 1: Self-Development

A good organization will take the time and resources necessary to ensure that its employees are always growing and becoming more skilled. Unfortunately, this is not always what happens. There are many reasons that an organization may not invest in the development of its employees. Due to the slacking economy, many organizations have found it more difficult to invest (financially) in their employees and have been forced to make decisions between investing in employee development and keeping the doors open. On the other hand, there are organizations and supervisors who simply do not see the value in investing in the development of their employees or believe they do not have the time. If the organization is unable to invest in an employee's development, does that mean that the employee will not be developed? The answer is NO!

In today's society, there is no reason for not engaging in self-development. All too often, people believe that they are unable to engage in career development because their supervisor does not support their development or the organization does not have the funds to invest in them. However, this is the wrong way to think about it. Since self-growth is vital to a successful person's career, they can refuse, as I do, to <u>not</u> be developed. Successful people know that they must invest in themselves, even if that means using their own money, vacation hours, or free time.

Successful people begin self-development by taking a good hard look at themselves. They can start by completing questionnaires such as the 360 Degree Assessment (which measures performance based on a range of coworkers' feedback), Myers-Briggs Type Indicator (MBTI; identifies personality preferences with a four-letter formula), and the Fundamental Interpersonal Relations Orientation (FIRO-B, which focuses on improving self-effectiveness and relationships with coworkers). These types of assessments provide successful people with insight into their strengths and areas of growth and can be found by visiting CPP.com.

Feedback. One of the most important tools that successful people use for self-development is feedback. Obtaining feedback from supervisors, coworkers, and other individuals provides successful people with real-time data of where they stand with their work tasks, insight into their strengths (and improvement areas), and most importantly, perceptions people have of them and their work. **Unfortunately, many people take feedback as a personal attack or as verification that they cannot perform that task. But, there is good news; as with most things in life, overcoming this obstacle is mental.** Changing our mindset about feedback may not be an easy task, but if we are willing to let go of our pride and focus on what is important, we will be able to gain information that could help further our career. People receive two types of feedback: positive and hostile.

Positive Feedback. Positive feedback is the feedback an individual hopes to receive. This type of feedback, referred to as "feed-forward" by <u>Marshal Goldsmith</u> (world-renowned author and executive coach), is focused on providing the recipient with information that will help him or her understand why the actions taken should be improved as well as how they can be improved in the future. This type of feedback tends to be fairly well accepted by individuals because it is less confrontational.

Hostile Feedback. On the contrary, hostile feedback focuses on what the individual has done wrong and does not provide information that helps the individual understand why his or her actions should be improved or how they can be improved in the future. Below is an example of hostile feedback and how one employee found a way to benefit from it.

Tina and Marcus have worked together for about 3 years. Though Tina recognizes Marcus as one of the smartest people she knows, for the first 2 years, Tina almost instantly became frustrated with Marcus when he gave her feedback. This was because Marcus had no problem saying that Tina was wrong and letting Tina know that he was right. It was not just what Marcus said that frustrated Tina; it was how he said it. Marcus's tone and nonverbal communication made Tina feel like she was incompetent. It was not until Tina realized that the success of her program was more important than her pride that she truly learned how to receive feedback from Marcus. Tina realized that Marcus's communication style seemed extremely confrontational, condescending, and was not going to change. Additionally, now that Tina knew Marcus better, she understood he wasn't trying to be mean. In fact, Marcus had saved Tina from embarrassment more than once.

However confrontational Marcus's communication style was, he had worked in this field for over 30 years and had a great deal of advice and expertise. Knowing that she could not change Marcus's communication style, Tina focused on changing her own mindset in order to take advantage of his expertise. From then on, Tina was conscious of her emotions when talking to Marcus. When Tina recognized that she was becoming agitated, she would think to herself, "This is who he is and how he communicates. If I become angry because of how he communicates, will that change anything?" The answer is no. Because there is no way to change Marcus, the most strategic way to deal with the situation is for Tina to focus on how she reacts to him. Instead of becoming agitated by Marcus's tone and delivery method, which could cause Tina to become angry and ultimately cloud her judgment, she began to focus on the content and gather the information that was helpful.

Marshall Goldsmith told a story in his book, *What Got You Here Won't Get You There,* about a man in a small boat heading upstream. The man sees a large boat heading towards him downstream. The man yells to the large boat to watch where it is going so that it does not hit him. Yet the boat continues its path towards him. The man, now extremely angry, yells again, "Watch where you are going! You are going to hit my boat!" Still the boat does not change its path. Eventually, the large boat collides with the small boat, forcing the man to jump out of his boat. The man is now infuriated and begins to violently yell at the boat. "What are you doing? You just destroyed my boat!" Soon after the accident, the man realizes that there is no one on the large boat. The boat had gotten loose from its port and had been floating downstream for miles. The man had been yelling at an empty boat. The man was mad at the boat for doing what boats do, floating with the stream. Instead of wasting his time trying to make the large boat change direction, the man could have changed the direction of his own boat so that it was not in the path of the large boat.

Using this story with the previous example, Tina being mad at Marcus for being Marcus does not make sense either. Once we understand that we cannot change others and that we should focus on what we can change about ourselves, it becomes much easier to take feedback from others, no matter how it is given. One final quote from Buddha relates to this topic: "Holding onto anger is like drinking poison and expecting the other person to die." The point is, being angry at others only hurts the individual holding the anger.

When working with others, results are dependent on the sum of an individual's actions and the actions of others (see Figure 7). As previously established, we cannot make others change; we only have control over ourselves and our actions. So, instead of focusing our efforts on trying to make someone see something our way in order to attain the desired result, the question should be asked, "What can I do to reach the goal?" or "What have I done to impede results?" Then ask yourself, "Why are the results important to me?" and ask the other person, "What results are important to you and why?" Try to figure out why the person is behaving the way he or she is and what behaviors you can change to make things smoother.

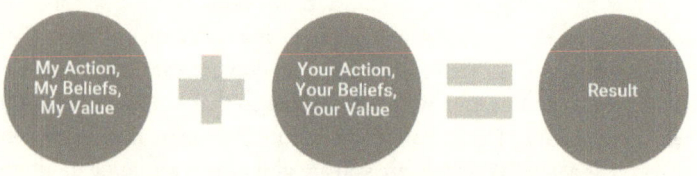

Figure 7. Personal accountability equation.

Ask for Feedback. Once we know how to accept feedback, we should begin asking for feedback from every possible source. Ask customers, supervisors, coworkers, mentors, collaborators, and anyone else who might have some useful input. We can also ask for feedback from people who may not like us. Asking for feedback from these different groups has three primary benefits. First, each person and group will have a different perspective of our work and will have different ideas as to how we can perform better. This does not suggest that we must believe and incorporate everything, but the feedback will provide us with a list of recommendations that can be considered when trying to improve ourselves and our programs.

> *"You don't have to do it all, you don't have to do it all right now, and you don't have to do it all by yourself."*
> —*Jeanne Meister*

Next, gaining feedback provides us with an insight into what people think about us and how they perceive our actions. The old quote

"What individuals define as real is real in its consequences"[3] still holds true today. People react to, and build perceptions on, what they believe is true, which can sometimes be the exact opposite of what is actually true. Successful people appreciate feedback on their actions and behaviors because it allows them the opportunity to make adjustments to their behaviors to realign their intended behavior with others' perceptions of their actions.

For example, Pam had a young employee, Lucy, who majored in a field that was not the primary focus of Pam's projects. Upon leaving the organization, Lucy wrote the meanest and most negative evaluation of Pam's performance that Pam had ever received because of this mismatch. Lucy described how Pam did not provide her with substantive work and was never at her desk. Additionally, Lucy said that she would have liked to have worked more with another supervisor, Tom, because he provided her work in her area of study.

Lucy had perceived Pam as a bad leader. However, the reality of the situation was that Lucy had not been assigned to Pam. Lucy's primary supervisor, Tom, did not have enough work to keep her busy, so Pam began asking around the office for projects that Lucy could work on. Though the projects were not in Lucy's area of study, they were tasks that needed to be completed and were of great importance to the office. Lucy did not realize how much time Pam spent trying to find tasks for her—time that was taking away from Pam's projects. Receiving the feedback from the intern taught Pam that perceptions are more real than reality. From then on, Pam made a conscious effort to adjust her behavior so that employees knew who their primary supervisor was and how much effort went into providing them with a valuable experience.

Finally, the third reason to ask for feedback from many different groups is that asking for feedback makes that individual feel important, valued, and *respected*. This is very beneficial in building positive perceptions for the successful person as an inclusive leader.

---

[3] Adapted from W. I. Thomas, 1928

Career Tip 2: Support Network

Developing a strong social network is another one of the most important steps successful people take to develop themselves. A social network can be developed on a few different levels. The first type is networking for name recognition. When looking to build name recognition, one might start by contacting individuals who are specialists in a particular field of interest. This can be done by using Google, LinkedIn, and other resources such as coworkers to identify those individuals. Once their contact information has been gathered, ask to meet them for lunch in order to begin establishing a relationship. During the lunch, or sometimes happy hour or dinner, we should do our best to keep the focus of the conversation on them and learn as much as possible.

The F.R.O.M. Method. A useful acronym for networking is "F.R.O.M." F, for Family, means that the first questions asked should be light, such as asking about the person's family. Other questions that fall into this category are where the individual is from and where he or she went to school. The second set of questions, R, should be geared towards what the individual does for Recreation. Talking about the first two categories should put the person in a positive frame of mind while also allowing the question asker to find similarities. This is the most important aspect of networking. Too many people enter into a conversation thinking that the most important thing is to talk about the technical aspects of the person's job. However, because there is no way that anyone can learn everything they want to know about a particular topic during the first conversation, it is more important to build relationships so that the individuals will want to connect again. Once the F and R have been addressed, questions can begin to address the Occupation (i.e., O). Lastly, questions can relate to M for Money (i.e., business-related issues).

"Do not wait; the time will never be right. Start where you stand, and work with whatever tools you may have at your command." —Napoleon Hill

Some individuals are hesitant to network because they fear that they will "say the wrong thing" or "look stupid." Using the F.R.O.M. method can reduce the individual's anxiety for two key reasons. First, the F.R.O.M. method teaches you to keep the conversation light-hearted and about the person with whom you are speaking. This means that you do not have to worry about "sounding smart" or being an expert in a specific field. Instead, you can focus on being friendly and learning everything possible about that person. Second, keeping the conversation centered on the other person gives you the opportunity to learn the person's mannerisms, communication style, topics of interest, and much more. This is all information that you can use to prepare for your next meeting.

Peer Mentoring Groups. Sometimes successful people identify an inner circle within their social group who will help with moral support. As high performers, successful people can easily find themselves physically and mentally drained from the work and extracurricular activities they participate in. One way to regain this strength, while also being able to continually engage in stimulating conversations, is to develop a peer mentoring group. This group, composed of other high performers from a diverse set of backgrounds, can provide successful persons with an outlet from an extremely busy career. This is an informal group of colleagues who meet up occasionally for dinner, a movie, bike riding, and other non–work-related activities. However, interacting with this group is a career development activity because it can allow opportunities to release stress built up during the week and bounce ideas off of individuals who are positive and want the individual to succeed in life as well as work. Additionally, because the group should be composed of individuals with diverse ways of thinking, successful people are able to receive many different types of suggestions and recommendations when they pose a question to the group.

Successful people develop their "Success Team," composed of members of their peer mentoring group who represent all areas important to their success. For example, a program manager for executive education needs to know how to manage a budget, write contracts, market the program, select speakers, and convince management to invest in the program. Instead of trying to become an expert in all of those areas, successful people find individuals who specialize in all of those areas so they can leverage the group's strengths to achieve the desired outcome. This same tactic can be used in personal life as well.

Career Tip 3: Take Responsibility for Your Decisions

When given the opportunity to work on new projects, successful people always take responsibility for their decisions, good or bad. This means that one should assess all of the pros and cons of a decision before acting. If the decision works out well, there is a high likelihood the average individual will be happy to take credit—but successful people will take responsibility even when the outcome is not positive. By taking responsibility for their actions, successful people show their leaders that they are mature in their thinking and can be trusted. Sometimes in order to perform a job effectively, the old saying "It's better to beg for forgiveness than ask permission" may apply. This means that actions taken are being done at a risk that may result in discipline. There will be times when everything works out and people are rewarded for their actions, but there will also be times when things do not go as planned and the people involved will need to admit what happened to their boss. Many bosses will appreciate that the individuals had the courage to stand by their actions.

Active vs. Passive. Taking responsibility for our actions also means that we make the decision to either *let* things happen to us or *make* things happen for us. The following exercises are similar but phrased differently to reflect both a passive and active method to a situation.

A. Exercise 1: Imagine that you have been working at your organization for 15 years and you are getting ready to take another job. At your going-away party, everyone is given the opportunity to say a few words about you. What would they say? What adjectives would they say most represented you? This is a very helpful exercise, if you are honest with yourself, because you are trying to look at yourself from another's perspective. This can provide insight into how others may perceive you. As stated earlier, it is always important that you know how others perceive you and your actions. However, this exercise would be slightly more helpful if phrased another way.

B. Exercise 2: Imagine that you have been working at your organization for 15 years and you are getting ready to take another job. At your going-away party, everyone is given the opportunity to say a few words about you. What would you want others to say about you? What adjectives would you want them to use to describe you? Asking yourself what you *want* others to think about you provides you with actionable information. Now you can ask yourself, "What can I do to make people think that about me?" and "How should I change or modify my behavior?" Once more, asking yourself these questions puts the onus back on the person you can most effectively control: you.

As you can see, in the first example, the approach is passive—waiting and wanting others to think in a certain way. Conversely, the approach in the second example is active—changing behavior, acting in a certain way, so that others will change their perceptions about you. By imagining this situation and asking yourself these questions regularly, you will be able to keep yourself on target toward a successful career.

WE MUST START TODAY

Throughout my life, I have had the opportunity to meet many wonderful people, some of whom have become my mentors. It was these people and the experiences that I encountered as a result of meeting them that helped me identify my ultimate goal and the best path to reach it. Learning the importance of identifying my concrete goals and taking the time to create detailed plans to achieve those goals have been crucial to my success thus far in life. But the one thing that we must always remember is that we are all different. We were raised differently, had different starting points, have different dreams, and are influenced by different people and circumstances throughout our lives. Because of this, we should not be afraid to use the plans that work best for us. The strategies outlined in this handbook are only a few of the many strategies that I have developed over the course of my life. However, with every conversation I have with other successful people, I learn new interesting and creative strategies for achieving goals and ensuring that my plans come to fruition. As successful people, we should be comfortable with who we are and do our best to fully utilize all of our strengths.

> *"To contemplate quitting is human. To persist and not give up is (what successful people do)."*
> —*Clifton Taulbert*

Lastly, if we do not take the first step we will never get any closer to reaching our goals. We cannot wait for the perfect situation to begin the journey. We must start today. Using the example goal statement and template in the appendix:

- Take a few minutes to identify one of your goals. (Be sure to ask yourself *why*.)
- Begin thinking about a plan for achieving that goal. (Be sure to use the methods outlined above.)
- What strategies can you put in place to start you on your path?
- What can you do today?
- Now go do it!

There are going to be times when you are faced with a detour or traffic that will slow you down in the pursuit of your goals, but you must never give up. Keep moving forward and making progress, and you will eventually overcome any challenge that may present itself. Good luck, and I want to help you reach your goals! Subscribe to my career and leadership development newsletter at AlexTremble.com.

The road to success is always under construction, but as long as you view the "road closures" as nothing more than a detour, you will find your way back on the right path. As long as you know where you are in relation to where you want to be, you can find a way to reach your goal.

RECOMMENDED RESOURCES

Goldsmith, M. (2007). *What got you here won't get you there: How successful people become even more successful.* New York, NY: Hyperion.

Goldsmith, M. (2009). *Mojo: How to get it, how to keep it, how to get it back if you lose it.* New York, NY: Hyperion.

Hedges, K. (2012). *The power of presence: Unlock your potential to influence and engage others.* New York, NY: American Management Association.

Meister, J. C., & Willyerd, K. (2010). *The 2020 workplace: How innovative companies attract, develop, and keep tomorrow's employees today.* New York, NY: HarperCollins.

Taulbert, C., & Schoeniger, G. (2010). *Who owns the ice house? Eight life lessons from an unlikely entrepreneur.* Cleveland, OH: ELI Press.

Ted Talks. http://www.ted.com/talks

APPENDIX:
Example Goal Statement and Template

■━━━━◆━━━━◆━━━━◆━━━━■

M y goal is to (DESCRIBE SPECIFIC GOAL) by (DATE). I want to achieve this goal because (STATE WHY THIS IS IMPORTANT TO YOU). In order to achieve this goal, I must accomplish all of the following: (LIST ALL PIT STOPS IDENTIFIED). I have researched all of my pit stops to identify any certifications, skills, experiences, networks, etc. required by or related to them. I am confident that I can realistically reach my pit stops prior to the date I want to have accomplished my goal. Below I have listed in more detail the particulars of my plan.

Goal: _____

_____

Timeframe: _____

_____

Pit stops: _____

_____

Pit Stop A. _____
    1. **Milestone** _____
        • **How long should it take?** _____
        • **How much money does it require?** _____
        • **Who can help me?** _____
        • **Planned completion date** _____

2. Milestone _____
   - How long should it take? _____
   - How much money does it require? _____
   - Who can help me? _____
   - Planned completion date _____

3. Milestone _____
   - How long should it take? _____
   - How much money does it require? _____
   - Who can help me? _____
   - Planned completion date _____

Pit Stop B. _____
   1. Milestone _____
      - How long should it take? _____
      - How much money does it require? _____
      - Who can help me? _____
      - Planned completion date _____

   2. Milestone _____
      - How long should it take? _____
      - How much money does it require? _____
      - Who can help me? _____
      - Planned completion date _____

Pit Stop C. _____
   1. Milestone _____
      - How long should it take? _____
      - How much money does it require? _____
      - Who can help me? _____
      - Planned completion date _____

   2. Milestone _____
      - How long should it take? _____
      - How much money does it require? _____
      - Who can help me? _____
      - Planned completion date _____

ABOUT THE AUTHOR

Alex Tremble is the founder and CEO of GPS Leadership Solutions, LLC, an organization dedicated to providing young professionals (i.e., high school students through mid-level employees) with the leadership, innovation, and goal-setting strategies necessary to excel in today's fast moving society.

Drawing from his own experiences with mentoring and managing federal executive leadership development programs, Alex dedicates a great deal of his life to ensuring that youth around the world are afforded the same mentoring and leadership development opportunities he was given as a young professional. To this end, he continues to actively seek opportunities to interact with and teach tomorrow's leaders. He was invited to speak at the 2013 White House Youth Summit, 2013 Maryland Future Business Leaders of America Conference, and 2013 D.C. Young Men's Conference, where he spoke on the importance of being intentional with one's life and social media networking.

Alex also spoke on "The Importance of Being Positive, Persistent, and Pliable" for the federally sponsored "GEAR UP" program and was nominated for the 2013 Emerging Training Leaders Award. In 2011 he was a panelist for The Washington Center's "Getting into the Federal Government for Young Professionals" discussion and served as a judge for the Maryland Distributive Education Club of America scholarship competition. Alex has spoken on behalf of federal agencies on topics such as employment in the public sector, leadership development, mentoring, and the importance of networking to develop one's career. Finally, Alex serves on the Alumni Association Board of Governors for the University of Baltimore and has written numerous leadership and self-development articles that have been internationally recognized.

Alex holds a B.A. in psychology and sociology from William Penn University (2008) and a master's degree in industrial and organizational psychology from the University of Baltimore (2011). He is originally from Victorville, CA.

Sign up for his career and leadership development newsletter at http://alextremble.com/. You can also contact or follow Alex D. Tremble at

> https://www.facebook.com/FederalCareerCoach/
> https://www.linkedin.com/in/alextremble/
> https://instagram.com/alexdtremble
> https://www.youtube.com/alextremble

www.ingramcontent.com/pod-product-compliance
Lightning Source LLC
Chambersburg PA
CBHW021445170526
45164CB00001B/395